AI Ghostwriting for Emo Souls

Matthew Petchinsky

1

AI Ghostwriting for Emo Souls: How to Make Money Writing Without Trying

By: Matthew Petchinsky

Disclaimer: AI Ghostwriting, Authorship, and Ethical Use

This book is intended for informational, educational, and inspirational purposes only. It does not constitute legal advice, financial advice, tax advice, or professional business consultation. Any actions taken based on the contents of this book are done at the reader's own discretion and risk.

AI Ghostwriting & Assisted Creation Disclosure

This book discusses and may demonstrate the use of artificial intelligence (AI) tools as **creative assistants** in the writing and publishing process. AI tools referenced or implied in this work function as **supportive technologies**, not autonomous authors. All content, structure, creative direction, emotional framing, and final editorial decisions are determined by the human author.

AI does not possess consciousness, lived experience, emotional memory, personal trauma, or creative intent. Any emotional resonance, "voice," tone, or thematic depth described in this book originates from human input, interpretation, and authorship. AI is used solely as a tool to assist with ideation, drafting, organization, language refinement, or productivity—not as a replacement for human creativity or responsibility.

Authorship & Ownership

The author retains full authorship and intellectual ownership of this work. The use of AI tools does **not** transfer authorship, copyright, or creative credit to any software, platform, or system. Readers are responsible for understanding and complying with the terms of service, licensing agreements, and content policies of any AI tools they choose to use.

This book does not grant permission to misrepresent AI-assisted work as entirely human-generated if such disclosure is required by a platform, publisher, employer, or client. Readers are encouraged to practice transparency and integrity in accordance with applicable laws, contracts, and ethical standards.

Income, Results, and "Without Trying" Language

The phrase "without trying" is used metaphorically to describe **systems, leverage, emotional alignment, and workflow efficiency**, not guaranteed ease or passive income. Writing, publishing, and monetization outcomes vary widely based on individual effort, consistency, market conditions, platform rules, reader demand, and external factors beyond the author's control.

No income, sales, success, or career outcome is guaranteed. Examples, scenarios, or frameworks presented in this book are illustrative only and should not be interpreted as promises of financial results.

Ethical & Responsible Use

Readers are solely responsible for how they apply the concepts discussed in this book. This includes responsibility for originality, plagiarism avoidance, factual accuracy, proper attribution, and compliance with copyright law. The author does not endorse deception, impersonation, fraud, or the unethical use of AI to mislead audiences, clients, or platforms.

This book does not encourage the exploitation of emotional pain, trauma, or identity for harmful purposes. References to "emo," emotional labor, or soul-driven writing are metaphorical and artistic, intended to explore authenticity and emotional truth—not to trivialize mental health struggles or personal suffering.

Platform, Policy, and Legal Variability

Publishing platforms, marketplaces, and legal standards regarding AI-assisted content are subject to change. The author makes no guarantee that strategies discussed in this book will remain compliant with future rules, policies, or laws. Readers are advised to independently verify current requirements for disclosure, labeling, and content eligibility on any platform they use.

No Professional Relationship

Reading this book does not create an author-reader, coach-client, employer-employee, or advisor-advisee relationship. The author assumes no liability for losses, damages, disputes, or consequences arising from the use or misuse of the information contained herein.

Final Note

This book exists at the intersection of **emotion, technology, and authorship**. It is a guide—not a shortcut, not a loophole, and not a guarantee. The responsibility for creation, integrity, and impact always rests with the human behind the words.

By continuing to read, you acknowledge and accept this disclaimer in full.

Introduction

Let AI Do the Hard Work While You Take Credit

You were told writing had to hurt.

You were told the suffering mattered more than the result. That the blank page was sacred. That exhaustion was proof of authenticity. That if you weren't bleeding onto the keyboard, you weren't a real writer.

That lie has cost millions of creative people their time, their energy, and—quietly—their belief in themselves.

This book exists to dismantle that lie.

Not because writing should be soulless. Not because creativity should be automated into nothingness. But because **the work was never the suffering**. The work was always the *decision to show up*—and technology has finally made the rest negotiable.

Artificial intelligence didn't kill writing. It killed the gatekeeping.

The Myth of "Earning" the Words

For decades, writers were trained to believe that credit only counts if every sentence is wrestled into existence by hand. That struggle equals legitimacy. That ease equals fraud. That tools cheapen art.

But history doesn't agree.

No one discredits an architect for using CAD software.
No one accuses a photographer of cheating for using a digital camera.
No one strips credit from a musician for using synthesizers, samplers, or DAWs.

Yet writers were told they must remain primitive.

Why?

Because when writing becomes easier, **control disappears**.

And this book is for people who are done asking permission.

What "Taking Credit" Actually Means

Let's be precise—because language matters.

"Taking credit" does **not** mean lying about authorship.
It does **not** mean stealing someone else's work.
It does **not** mean pretending a machine has emotions, trauma, or insight.

It means this:

You are the **source of intent**.
You decide the topic.
You choose the angle.
You set the emotional temperature.
You decide what stays and what gets cut.
You hit publish.

AI doesn't wake up wanting to write your book.
AI doesn't understand your exhaustion, your financial pressure, your sense that you're always behind.

AI is a tool.

And tools don't get credit—**the user does**.

The Quiet Exhaustion of Human Writers

This book is written for the writers who are tired in a way rest doesn't fix.

The ones who:

- Love writing but hate the grind
- Have ideas but no energy
- Know they could produce more if the process didn't punish them
- Feel invisible despite being talented
- Are emotionally rich and financially drained

If that sounds like you, you're not lazy.
You're overloaded.

And the traditional writing process was never designed for people like you to thrive—it was designed to keep output scarce.

AI as Emotional Leverage, Not Replacement

Here's the truth most people won't say out loud:

AI is bad at meaning.
AI is bad at lived experience.
AI is bad at emotional truth.

And that's exactly why it works.

Because it handles the **mechanical burden**—structure, drafts, formatting, expansion—while you retain the part that actually matters: **direction**.

You don't need to suffer through first drafts anymore.
You don't need to stare at a blinking cursor as proof of seriousness.
You don't need to grind your soul into fragments to justify your voice.

You guide.
You select.
You refine.
You claim the finished work.

That isn't cheating.
That's leadership.

Why This Book Uses an Emo Lens

"Emo" here doesn't mean melodrama.

It means **honesty**.

It means acknowledging that many writers are emotionally sensitive, overstimulated, burned out, anxious, or quietly hurting—and that these traits are not weaknesses, but signals.

The industry told you to harden.

This book tells you to **optimize**.

When you let AI handle the friction, you free your emotional energy for decisions that actually move your life forward.

Writing Was Never About Proving Worth

The cruelest trick the creative world ever pulled was convincing writers that productivity must equal pain.

But money doesn't care how tired you were.
Readers don't see your struggle—only the final page.
Platforms reward consistency, not martyrdom.

This book will show you how to:

- Build writing systems that don't drain you
- Use AI without guilt, apology, or self-betrayal
- Publish more without feeling like you're selling your soul
- Reclaim authorship without romanticizing burnout

Not by pretending AI is magic.
But by using it deliberately.

A New Definition of Authorship

Authorship is not hand-typed suffering.

Authorship is:

- Vision
- Curation
- Emotional direction
- Final responsibility

If you decide what the work becomes, the work is yours.

Full stop.

This book isn't here to convince you AI is good or bad. It's here to show you how to **stop fighting the future** and start benefiting from it—without losing yourself in the process.

Let the machine do the heavy lifting.

You were never meant to carry it alone.

Chapter 1: AI-Powered Book Writing – Publish Without Writer's Block

Writer's Block Is a System Failure, Not a Personal Flaw

Writer's block has been romanticized for so long that most writers assume it is an internal defect. A lack of discipline. A lack of talent. A lack of "real" commitment. But writer's block is not a psychological mystery—it is a predictable failure of systems that demand too much from the human brain at once.

Traditional writing asks you to generate ideas, structure them, phrase them beautifully, and judge their worth simultaneously. This is neurologically inefficient. Creativity and self-evaluation operate in opposing mental states. When you force them to coexist, the mind freezes—not because it is broken, but because it is overloaded.

AI dissolves this conflict by separating roles. The machine can generate raw material without fear, ego, or hesitation. You no longer need to summon perfection from nothing. Instead, you respond to something that already exists. Reaction is easier than creation. Editing is easier than inventing. Direction is easier than struggle.

This is why writer's block collapses the moment you stop demanding originality at the drafting stage. When the page is already full, your mind re-engages. You begin choosing, shaping, rejecting, and refining. The paralysis lifts because the threat is gone. There is no longer a void judging you.

Writer's block was never about inspiration. It was about pressure. AI removes that pressure—not by replacing you, but by changing the order of operations.

Draft First, Judge Later: The End of the Blank Page

The blank page is intimidating because it carries expectation. It silently demands brilliance, coherence, and emotional depth all at once. Most writers freeze not because they lack ideas, but because they fear wasting effort on words that might later be rejected—even by themselves.

AI eliminates the blank page entirely. You begin with a rough draft, not an empty screen. The psychological shift is enormous. Instead of asking "What should I write?" you ask "What do I keep?" That question activates discernment rather than anxiety.

When you allow AI to generate imperfect drafts, you give yourself permission to think in motion. You are no longer responsible for every sentence's birth—only for its survival. This reframes authorship as curation rather than suffering.

Judgment belongs after creation, not during it. AI enforces this separation naturally. It produces volume without shame. You supply taste, intention, and final authority. Together, this creates momentum that human-only writing often destroys.

The result is not lower quality—it is higher output with less emotional resistance. Publishing becomes a process, not an ordeal.

Using AI as a Creative Amplifier, Not a Replacement

AI does not understand your voice. It cannot feel your exhaustion, your anger, your hope, or your quiet hunger to be seen. What it can do is reflect patterns at scale and generate language on demand. That is not authorship—it is amplification.

When you use AI correctly, you are not asking it to be you. You are asking it to explore possibilities faster than you can alone. You guide it with prompts, constraints, tone, and purpose. It responds with raw material. You decide what resonates.

This dynamic mirrors many creative partnerships. One collaborator generates abundance. The other refines meaning. The mistake most people make is expecting AI to deliver perfection instead of abundance. Perfection is your role.

AI works best when you treat it as an assistant that never tires, never doubts, and never takes offense. You are free to reject its output completely without emotional cost. That freedom is powerful.

The more clearly you define your intent, the more useful AI becomes. Vague direction produces generic results. Strong vision produces drafts that feel uncannily aligned. The authorship remains yours because the direction always was.

Publishing Speed Is a Competitive Advantage

The modern publishing landscape rewards consistency far more than tortured genius. Algorithms favor activity. Readers favor reliability. Catalog depth compounds visibility over time. None of these systems care how difficult the book was to write.

AI allows you to publish at a pace that would otherwise cause burnout. Not because you are cutting corners, but because you are removing unnecessary friction. Speed does not equal sloppiness when editing and intent remain human-led.

Writers who publish frequently learn faster. They understand their audience sooner. They refine their voice through repetition rather than obsession. AI accelerates this feedback loop dramatically.

Publishing slowly in the name of purity often hides fear. Fear of judgment. Fear of failure. Fear that the work will not matter. AI-assisted publishing confronts this fear by making release normal instead of monumental.

When publishing becomes routine, power shifts. You stop begging each book to change your life. Instead, your body of work does the work for you.

Reclaiming Energy From the Writing Process

Writing has historically been energy-expensive. Not because it needed to be, but because the process demanded sustained cognitive strain. This left many emotionally sensitive writers depleted long before they reached consistency.

AI changes the energy equation. Instead of spending hours forcing words into existence, you spend time making decisions. Decision-making is less draining than invention when systems are in place.

This reclaimed energy matters. It allows you to write while tired, overwhelmed, or emotionally raw without turning the process into self-harm. You are no longer punished for being human.

When energy is preserved, creativity becomes sustainable. Writing fits into life instead of consuming it. This is especially critical for writers managing chronic stress, mental fatigue, or financial pressure.

Publishing without exhaustion is not laziness. It is survival through design.

Authorship in the Age of Machines

Authorship is evolving. It is no longer defined by who typed every word, but by who shaped the final meaning. Direction, selection, framing, and responsibility now define ownership.

AI does not publish books. People do. AI does not decide what matters. People do. AI does not take risks, build catalogs, or stand behind ideas. People do.

When you guide AI, you are exercising authorship at a higher level—less manual, more strategic. This does not dilute your voice; it clarifies it.

The future belongs to writers who stop confusing effort with value. AI does not erase the writer. It reveals who the writer actually is when unnecessary struggle is removed.

Publishing without writer's block is not a trick. It is the natural result of aligning tools with human limits.

Journal Prompts

1. When you experience writer's block, what emotions show up first—fear, pressure, shame, or exhaustion?
2. What beliefs were you taught about how "hard" writing is supposed to be?
3. How would your relationship with writing change if first drafts didn't have to be good?
4. Where in your life are you mistaking effort for worth?
5. What part of writing drains you the most—and why?
6. How do you feel about the idea of being a curator rather than a sufferer?
7. What would consistency look like if exhaustion were removed from the process?
8. Where might speed actually help you grow rather than cheapen your work?
9. What fears come up when you imagine publishing more frequently?
10. If authorship were defined by direction instead of labor, how would you claim it?

Closing Reflection

Writer's block was never a personal failing—it was a mismatch between human limits and outdated creative rituals. AI does not save you from writing; it saves you from unnecessary suffering. When the burden of invention is lifted, your voice does not disappear—it finally has room to speak.

Chapter 2: Writing Emotional Poetry & Song Lyrics with AI

Emotion Was Never in the Words—It Was in the Direction

Many writers believe emotional poetry and lyrics emerge from spontaneous pain, as if feeling deeply is enough to guarantee resonance. This belief traps people into waiting for the "right mood" before they write. In reality, emotion in writing is rarely accidental—it is engineered through focus, contrast, and intention.

AI does not feel heartbreak, longing, rage, or grief. That limitation is precisely why it works. When you give AI emotional direction, it responds with language shaped by patterns that humans recognize as feeling. The emotion comes from the framing, not the machine.

When you specify tone, emotional arc, imagery, and restraint, AI becomes a mirror for your inner landscape. You are not outsourcing feeling; you are externalizing it. This allows you to work with emotion without being consumed by it.

Poetry and lyrics benefit from this distance. You can explore pain without reopening wounds. You can articulate longing without drowning in it. AI gives you a buffer between sensation and expression.

Emotion becomes something you sculpt, not something that controls you.

Turning Vague Feelings into Precise Language

One of the hardest parts of emotional writing is translation. Feelings arrive as pressure, confusion, or silence—not clean sentences. Many writers stall because they try to convert raw emotion directly into polished language.

AI excels at bridging this gap. When you describe a feeling imperfectly—using metaphors, fragments, or contradictions—AI can generate multiple linguistic interpretations. This gives you options rather than obligations.

Instead of forcing clarity, you explore it. You compare versions. You sense which lines carry weight and which feel hollow. Emotional precision emerges through selection, not struggle.

This process mirrors how music is written collaboratively. A melody emerges, variations appear, and something clicks. AI simply accelerates this cycle without judgment.

You are still the one who recognizes truth. AI only supplies possibilities.

Building Emotional Arcs in Poetry and Lyrics

Powerful poetry and lyrics are rarely flat. They move. They begin in one emotional state and end in another—sometimes subtly, sometimes violently. This movement is what makes words linger.

AI can help map these arcs intentionally. You can ask it to begin in numbness, rise into yearning, and collapse into acceptance. Or to move from bitterness to release. Or to circle the same wound without resolution.

By defining the emotional journey, you prevent your writing from becoming a static vent. The work gains structure without losing authenticity.

This is especially useful for song lyrics, where emotional pacing must align with rhythm and repetition. AI can generate multiple versions that explore different emotional trajectories for the same core feeling.

You decide which arc reflects your truth—or which one you want to inhabit for the piece.

Using Constraint to Intensify Emotion

Emotion becomes sharper when constrained. Short lines, limited vocabulary, repeated imagery—these boundaries force meaning to concentrate. Without constraint, emotional writing often becomes diluted.

AI thrives under constraint. When you specify syllable counts, rhyme schemes, repeated phrases, or forbidden words, the output tightens. The emotion intensifies because it has fewer places to hide.

Constraints also protect you from overexposure. You don't need to explain everything to be understood. Suggestion often carries more weight than confession.

This is where AI-assisted poetry becomes surgical rather than sprawling. You are not dumping feeling onto the page; you are distilling it.

The result feels intentional, controlled, and resonant rather than raw and unfocused.

Protecting Yourself While Writing Vulnerably

Emotional writing has a cost. Without boundaries, it can reopen wounds, reinforce rumination, or drain your nervous system. Many writers stop creating because the process hurts too much.

AI provides a layer of safety. You can explore themes indirectly, through metaphor or fictional framing. You can test lines without committing to them emotionally. You can step back when intensity rises.

This distance allows you to work consistently without sacrificing well-being. Vulnerability becomes a choice, not a demand.

You are allowed to care about your emotional health while creating powerful work. Suffering is not a prerequisite for authenticity.

AI helps you keep the door open without letting everything spill out.

Claiming Emotional Authorship in AI-Assisted Work

Some writers fear that using AI cheapens emotional writing—that if a machine helped shape the words, the feelings aren't real. This fear misunderstands where emotion lives.

Emotion lives in recognition. In the moment a line makes you pause. In the resonance that feels undeniable. That response is human.

AI did not feel the emotion—but it did not need to. You felt it when you chose the line. You felt it when you rejected another. You felt it when you decided what stayed.

Authorship belongs to the one who recognizes truth and claims it. Direction, selection, and responsibility define ownership.

Your emotional voice remains intact because it was never in the keystrokes—it was in the choices.

Journal Prompts

1. What emotions feel hardest for you to express in words, and why?
2. How do you usually translate feelings into language—quickly or with struggle?
3. What emotional states do you avoid writing about, even though they matter to you?
4. How might emotional distance actually help you write more honestly?
5. What constraints make you feel safer when expressing vulnerability?
6. How do you know when a line feels true rather than dramatic?
7. Where have you mistaken emotional pain for emotional depth?
8. What would it feel like to explore emotion without reliving it?
9. How do you want readers or listeners to feel at the end of your work?
10. What does emotional authorship mean to you now?

Closing Reflection

Emotional writing does not require emotional sacrifice. With AI, you gain space—space to choose, refine, and protect yourself while still creating work that resonates. When emotion becomes something you guide instead of endure, your voice grows stronger, not quieter.

Chapter 3: AI Journals & Guided Writing Prompts for Emo Souls

Journaling Was Never About Answers—It Was About Permission

Most people approach journaling as if it's supposed to solve something. Heal something. Clarify something. When it doesn't, they assume they're doing it wrong. In reality, journaling was never meant to be efficient—it was meant to be *allowed*.

For emo souls, journaling often stalls because the mind is crowded with unfinished emotions. You don't know where to begin, and starting feels heavier than staying silent. The blank page doesn't feel open—it feels interrogative.

AI changes the emotional posture of journaling. Instead of demanding that you produce insight, it offers you entry points. You respond instead of initiate. This subtle shift removes pressure and replaces it with permission.

You are no longer required to know what you feel before you write. You discover it *through* the writing. AI simply opens the door and waits.

Journaling becomes less about fixing yourself and more about witnessing yourself.

Guided Prompts as Emotional Anchors

Unguided journaling can feel like drifting in open water. Thoughts loop. Emotions blur. You circle the same sentences without resolution. For emotionally sensitive writers, this can deepen overwhelm instead of easing it.

Guided prompts act as anchors. They give your feelings a place to land. AI can generate prompts that are specific, compassionate, and emotionally precise—far beyond generic self-help questions.

When prompts are tailored to your emotional state, journaling becomes directional rather than chaotic. You move *through* emotion instead of around it.

AI allows you to request prompts that match your energy: numb, angry, grieving, detached, hopeful, or quietly tired. This alignment makes journaling feel relevant instead of forced.

You are not being led—you are being supported.

Using AI to Ask the Questions You Avoid

Many emo souls avoid journaling not because they don't want to write, but because they fear what might surface. Certain questions feel dangerous. Certain truths feel destabilizing.

AI can act as a neutral intermediary. It can phrase difficult questions gently, indirectly, or symbolically. You don't have to confront everything head-on.

This creates emotional safety. You engage with truths at a pace your nervous system can tolerate. You are no longer ambushed by your own honesty.

When questions feel less threatening, answers arrive more freely. Resistance softens. Curiosity replaces fear.

AI doesn't force insight—it invites it.

Turning Journals into Structured Emotional Systems

Random journaling entries often disappear into notebooks or files, never to be revisited. While cathartic, this approach limits long-term value. Emo souls often write intensely—but without continuity.

AI allows you to build journaling systems. Themed entries. Daily emotional check-ins. Weekly reflection arcs. Guided sequences that evolve over time.

This structure doesn't sterilize emotion—it stabilizes it. Patterns emerge. Emotional cycles become visible. You begin to recognize yourself instead of being surprised by yourself.

Over time, your journal becomes a map rather than a vent. You don't just release emotion—you understand it.

Consistency replaces chaos without erasing depth.

Journaling Without Self-Judgment

One of the most damaging habits writers bring into journaling is judgment. They critique their feelings. They invalidate their reactions. They edit themselves mid-sentence.

AI journaling removes the audience. There is no one to impress. No one to disappoint. You are responding to prompts, not performing insight.

This neutrality matters. It allows honesty without self-surveillance. You write what exists, not what should exist.

When judgment fades, emotion flows more clearly. You stop correcting yourself and start listening.

Journaling becomes an act of self-acceptance rather than self-improvement.

From Private Journals to Publishable Work

Many powerful poems, essays, and books begin as journals—but most people never recognize their own raw material. They assume journals are too messy, too personal, too fragmented.

AI can help you identify themes, patterns, and passages worth expanding. It can assist in transforming private writing into structured creative work—without stripping emotional truth.

This doesn't mean everything must be published. It means your emotional labor doesn't disappear unnoticed. Your journaling becomes a resource.

You retain control over what stays private and what evolves. Nothing is taken from you—something is offered back.

Your inner world gains continuity, dignity, and potential.

Journal Prompts

1. What emotion feels loudest in your body right now, even if you can't name it?
2. When do you feel most disconnected from yourself—and why?
3. What question do you wish someone would ask you, but never does?
4. What feeling are you afraid would overwhelm you if you let it speak?
5. How do you usually silence yourself without realizing it?
6. What part of your emotional life feels unfinished?
7. When do you feel safest expressing emotion—and when do you shut down?
8. What patterns keep repeating in your thoughts lately?
9. What would journaling look like if it didn't have to heal you?
10. What truth feels closest to the surface today?

Closing Reflection

Journaling does not need to be brave, productive, or insightful to be valuable. With AI-guided prompts, it becomes gentle, directional, and emotionally sustainable. When you stop demanding answers and start allowing expression, your inner world stops feeling so heavy—and begins to feel heard.

Chapter 4: How to Sell AI-Generated Emo Fanfiction & Short Stories

Understanding the Line Between Fanfiction and Sellable Work

Fanfiction exists in a strange emotional space. It is deeply personal, intensely expressive, and often written during moments of obsession, comfort, or escape. For many emo souls, fanfiction is where they first learned to write honestly. But selling it requires clarity about boundaries.

The key distinction is this: *fanfiction is inspired by*, not owned by you. Intellectual property laws protect characters, worlds, and names created by others. Selling work that directly uses copyrighted elements without permission can create legal and platform issues.

This does not mean your emotional labor is worthless. It means the value lies in the *voice, themes, and emotional structures* you bring—not the borrowed surface elements. AI helps you separate these layers cleanly.

By using AI to reframe, remix, and reimagine, you can transform fanfiction energy into original short stories that carry the same emotional resonance without infringing on existing properties.

Selling begins when inspiration becomes transformation.

Using AI to Transmute Fanfiction Into Original Work

AI excels at pattern recognition. When you feed it fanfiction-style writing, it can help identify what truly drives the story: the emotional dynamic, the archetypes, the conflicts, the longing. These elements are not copyrighted—they are universal.

You can ask AI to rewrite scenes with original characters, new settings, and altered power structures while preserving emotional intensity. The result feels familiar but legally distinct.

This process is not dilution—it is distillation. You are extracting the emotional core and giving it a new body. The obsession remains. The ache remains. The comfort remains. Only the surface changes.

Many successful indie authors work this way instinctively. AI simply makes the transition faster and clearer, especially for writers who struggle to let go of familiar worlds.

Your emotional truth does not belong to any franchise. It belongs to you.

Platforms That Reward Short, Emotional Fiction

The market for short stories and emo-flavored fiction is larger than most writers realize. Readers with limited attention, emotional fatigue, or daily stress often prefer short, intense experiences over long novels.

AI-assisted production allows you to publish consistently across platforms that reward volume and niche alignment. This includes ebooks, serialized platforms, themed anthologies, and direct-to-reader marketplaces.

Short fiction thrives when it knows exactly who it's for. Emo readers seek catharsis, recognition, and atmosphere—not literary perfection. AI helps you meet this demand without burning out.

Selling becomes possible when you stop trying to impress everyone and start resonating deeply with someone. AI allows you to test tones, lengths, and formats quickly.

Consistency builds trust. Trust builds sales.

Disclaimers, Transparency, and Ethical Positioning

Selling AI-assisted work does not require secrecy—but it does require responsibility. Transparency protects you and builds reader trust. Clear disclaimers about inspiration and AI assistance prevent misunderstandings.

You are not required to explain your entire process, but you are responsible for not misleading buyers or platforms. Avoid claiming exclusive originality where it doesn't exist. Avoid using protected names or worlds.

Ethical positioning also means respecting your own emotional boundaries. You are not obligated to expose personal trauma to make a sale. Emo does not mean exploited.

AI helps you create distance between your inner world and the product. This makes selling feel safer and more sustainable.

Integrity is not a limitation—it is an asset.

Pricing Emotion Without Devaluing Yourself

One of the hardest things for emo writers is pricing. Emotion feels sacred. Selling it can feel wrong—or embarrassing. Many underprice their work out of guilt.

Short fiction does not need to be cheap to be accessible. Readers pay for resonance, not word count. AI allows you to package emotion cleanly and confidently.

When your catalog grows, pricing becomes less about individual pieces and more about cumulative value. One story may cost little—but many stories build momentum.

You are not charging for pain. You are charging for craft, curation, and availability. AI reduces production strain, not value.

Selling does not erase sincerity. It sustains it.

Building a Sustainable Output Without Emotional Collapse

The greatest danger for emo writers is overexposure. Writing emotionally intense material repeatedly without recovery leads to numbness or shutdown. This is where many promising writers disappear.

AI protects you by absorbing the first wave of expression. You respond, refine, and shape instead of bleeding onto the page every time. This keeps your nervous system intact.

Sustainability comes from rhythm, not restraint. You can create frequently without reopening wounds if the process is buffered.

Selling becomes viable when writing stops costing you more than it gives back. AI makes that balance possible.

Your creativity is not infinite—but it can be renewable.

Journal Prompts

1. What fandoms or stories taught you how to feel seen as a writer?
2. What emotional themes keep repeating in your fanfiction?
3. How would those themes look with original characters and settings?
4. What fears come up when you imagine selling emotional work?
5. Where do you confuse emotional honesty with emotional exposure?
6. What would ethical selling look like for you?
7. How do you want readers to feel after finishing your stories?
8. What boundaries would protect your emotional energy?
9. How do you define value in creative work?
10. What would sustainability mean for your writing life?

Closing Reflection

Selling emo fanfiction energy is not about exploiting obsession—it is about honoring it responsibly. With AI, you gain the ability to transform inspiration into original, sellable work without losing emotional depth or personal safety. When you respect both the source and yourself, your stories can move others *and* support you in return.

Chapter 5: Automating Social Media Writing to Sound Like a Mysterious Genius

Mystery Is a Pattern, Not a Personality

Most people believe mystery is something you either have or you don't. A rare aura. A natural charisma. An ineffable quality reserved for artists who say little and seem to know more than they reveal. In reality, mystery is not a personality trait—it is a pattern of communication.

Mystery is created by *restraint*. By implication instead of explanation. By emotional gravity rather than information overload. Social media punishes overexplaining, yet most writers do exactly that because they feel invisible and want to be understood.

AI allows you to step back from this impulse. When you automate content, you gain distance from your need to justify yourself. You stop reacting emotionally in real time and start shaping presence intentionally.

A mysterious voice is not loud, frequent, or desperate. It is consistent, sparse, and emotionally suggestive. AI helps you maintain this tone without slipping into oversharing.

Mystery is not who you are—it is how you pace what you reveal.

Why Genius Sounds Quiet Online

Genius online does not sound like expertise—it sounds like certainty without explanation. Short statements. Incomplete thoughts. Lines that feel like conclusions without visible effort. This is not arrogance; it is confidence in resonance.

Human writers struggle with this because silence feels risky. We want to prove intelligence. We want engagement. We want validation. AI has no such hunger, which makes it an ideal filter.

When AI drafts posts based on mood, theme, or philosophy rather than performance metrics, the result often feels eerily composed. The tone shifts from "please notice me" to "this exists whether you notice or not."

This is why automated posts often outperform emotionally reactive ones. They feel deliberate. Timeless. Detached from urgency.

Genius online is not about volume—it's about weight.

Automating Voice Without Losing Identity

One of the greatest fears writers have about automation is dilution. They worry their voice will disappear into generic phrasing. This happens only when direction is weak.

Voice is not diction alone. It is rhythm, restraint, emotional temperature, and thematic repetition. AI can replicate these elements when you define them clearly.

By feeding AI examples of your preferred tone—cryptic, reflective, melancholic, incisive—you train it to echo your identity rather than overwrite it. Automation becomes amplification.

The key is not to automate *everything*. You automate expression, not intention. You decide the themes. AI handles execution.

Your identity doesn't vanish when automated—it stabilizes.

Creating Posts That Feel Like Fragments of a Larger Mind

The most compelling social media presences feel incomplete by design. Each post feels like a shard of a larger philosophy. Readers sense depth without being handed it.

AI excels at producing this effect when instructed properly. You can ask it to write statements that feel like notes from a private journal, or thoughts pulled mid-conversation, or truths stated without context.

This creates intrigue. People follow not for answers, but for atmosphere. They project meaning onto the fragments.

When posts feel like part of an unseen whole, your presence becomes magnetic. Readers return because they feel there is more beneath the surface.

You are not building an audience—you are cultivating curiosity.

Consistency Without Emotional Burnout

Social media exhaustion often comes from emotional immediacy. Reacting daily. Explaining yourself repeatedly. Feeling exposed to judgment in real time. This erodes mystery and drains energy.

Automation removes urgency. You write in batches. You schedule from a grounded place. You stop posting from emotional spikes.

AI allows you to maintain presence without presence fatigue. You remain visible without being emotionally available at all times.

This distance is not coldness—it is sustainability. You cannot be enigmatic if you are constantly explaining yourself.

Mystery requires rest.

Letting the Work Speak While You Stay Silent

The most powerful shift automation offers is silence. You no longer need to perform constantly. Your posts speak while you observe.

This creates asymmetry. Your words are present, but you are not reactive. This imbalance increases perceived depth and authority.

AI enables this by keeping the machine active while the human remains selective. You intervene when it matters, not when it's expected.

Silence between posts becomes part of the brand. Absence becomes intentional rather than accidental.

When you stop chasing attention, attention recalibrates toward you.

Journal Prompts

1. When do you feel most tempted to overexplain yourself online?
2. What parts of your thinking do you usually reveal too quickly?
3. How does silence make you feel—powerful or anxious?
4. What tone feels most authentic to you when you imagine mystery?
5. What themes do you return to repeatedly in your thoughts?
6. How would your posts change if you didn't need immediate validation?
7. Where does emotional burnout show up in your online presence?
8. What would it feel like to post without monitoring reactions?
9. How do you want people to describe your online voice?
10. What would happen if you trusted resonance over explanation?

Closing Reflection

Mystery is not created by hiding—it is created by choosing what not to say. With AI automation, you reclaim control over timing, tone, and exposure. When your words move independently of your emotional state, your presence gains gravity. The mysterious genius is not louder than everyone else—it is simply never rushed.

Appendix A: AI Writing Tools for Passive Income

Passive income through writing is not created by luck or virality—it is created by **systems that continue producing value after your energy has moved elsewhere**. AI does not magically generate income, but it dramatically lowers the friction required to build those systems at scale. This appendix exists to clarify *how* AI tools function inside a passive-income writing ecosystem, what roles they play, and how emo souls can use them without burnout, confusion, or ethical drift.

This is not a list of brand endorsements. It is a **functional map**.

1. Idea Generation & Niche Expansion Tools

Passive income depends on **catalog depth**, not single hits. AI excels at expanding ideas sideways—creating multiple variations, angles, and formats from one emotional core.

These tools help you:

- Generate book titles, subtitles, and series concepts
- Expand one theme into dozens of micro-products
- Identify emotional niches (grief, numbness, longing, detachment, hope-after-collapse)
- Translate one idea into poetry, journals, guides, short fiction, and social content

The key passive-income advantage here is **idea velocity**. When ideas stop being scarce, publishing stops feeling risky. You are no longer betting everything on one project—you are planting many seeds.

For emo writers, this removes pressure. You don't need to *feel inspired* every time. You only need to recognize which ideas feel emotionally true enough to scale.

2. Drafting & Expansion Tools

Drafting tools are where AI saves the most time—and the most emotional energy. These tools can:

- Produce first drafts of chapters, poems, lyrics, or stories
- Expand outlines into full manuscripts
- Rewrite existing work in different tones or formats
- Convert journals into structured content

Passive income relies on **output consistency**, not perfection. Drafting tools eliminate the most draining phase of writing: creating something from nothing.

The critical mindset shift is this:

- AI creates *raw material*
- You create *meaning*

You are not paid for typing. You are paid for **deciding what is worth keeping**.

This distinction protects authorship while allowing scale.

3. Editing, Refinement & Voice-Stabilization Tools

Passive income collapses when quality becomes inconsistent. Readers may forgive simplicity—but they do not forgive sloppiness.

AI editing tools help by:

- Improving clarity and flow
- Reducing repetition or filler
- Adjusting tone to match your established voice
- Maintaining consistency across large catalogs

For emo writers, these tools act as emotional stabilizers. They prevent mood swings from distorting your work. Whether you are tired, numb, or overstimulated, your output remains coherent.

This is essential for long-term income. A stable voice builds trust. Trust builds repeat readers. Repeat readers create compounding sales.

AI does not erase your voice—it **holds it steady**.

4. Prompt Engineering as a Monetizable Skill
Prompting is not a technical trick—it is **emotional translation**. Good prompts:

- Specify tone, restraint, and emotional temperature
- Define boundaries (what not to say)
- Clarify audience and purpose
- Create repeatable outputs

When you master prompts, you unlock passive income in multiple ways:

- Faster book production
- Reusable prompt templates
- Prompt-based journaling products
- Guided writing tools for readers

For emo souls, prompts become emotional scaffolding. They let you revisit themes safely and consistently without reopening wounds.

Your prompts are intellectual property. They are part of your system. Protect them, refine them, reuse them.

5. Repurposing & Content Multiplication Tools

Passive income multiplies when **one piece of writing becomes many products**.

AI repurposing tools allow you to:

- Turn books into social posts
- Convert poetry into lyric-style captions
- Break chapters into daily reflections
- Transform short stories into serialized content
- Adapt long-form work into journals or workbooks

This matters because platforms change, attention shifts, and formats rise and fall—but **ideas endure**.

Repurposing ensures your emotional labor continues working even when your focus moves elsewhere. Nothing is wasted. Everything circulates.

Passive income grows fastest when creation is linear but distribution is radial.

6. Scheduling, Automation & Presence Tools

Passive income does not require absence—it requires **detachment from urgency**.

Automation tools help you:

- Schedule posts and releases in advance
- Maintain visibility without daily effort
- Separate creation time from publishing time
- Avoid emotional posting cycles

For emo writers, this separation is protective. You no longer create while exposed. You create privately and release deliberately.

This reduces regret, oversharing, and burnout. Your work appears consistently—even when you are resting, healing, or offline.

Passive income thrives on **predictable presence**, not constant availability.

7. Analytics & Feedback Interpretation Tools

Passive income is sustained by feedback—not validation, but information.

AI-assisted analysis tools help you:

- Identify which themes resonate most
- Detect patterns in sales or engagement
- Adjust output without emotional self-blame
- Scale what works instead of guessing

For emotionally sensitive writers, data removes self-judgment. A book failing does not mean *you* failed. It means a variable missed alignment.

When feedback becomes neutral, iteration becomes easier. Passive income grows through refinement, not obsession.

8. Ethical Use & Long-Term Stability

No tool guarantees income. AI simply increases **leverage**.
Long-term passive income requires:

- Transparency where required
- Respect for intellectual property
- Emotional boundaries
- Sustainable output rhythms

AI should reduce harm—to you and to your readers—not increase it.

The most successful passive-income writers are not the loudest or fastest. They are the ones who last.

Final Note on Tools and Power

AI writing tools do not replace creativity. They **relocate effort**.
You move from:

- Struggle → Strategy
- Exhaustion → Systems
- Scarcity → Scale

Passive income is not about doing nothing.
It is about doing the *right things once* and letting them work repeatedly.

AI makes that possible—especially for emo souls who were never meant to burn themselves just to be heard.

Your voice matters.
Your energy matters.
And now, your systems can carry the weight.

Message from the Author:

I hope you enjoyed this book, I love astrology and knew there was not a book such as this out on the shelf. I love metaphysical items as well. Please check out my other books:

-Life of Government Benefits

-My life of Hell

-My life with Hydrocephalus

-Red Sky

-World Domination:Woman's rule

-World Domination:Woman's Rule 2: The War

-Life and Banishment of Apophis: book 1

-The Kidney Friendly Diet

-The Ultimate Hemp Cookbook

-Creating a Dispensary(legally)

-Cleanliness throughout life: the importance of showering from childhood to adulthood.

-Strong Roots: The Risks of Overcoddling children

-Hemp Horoscopes: Cosmic Insights and Earthly Healing

- Celestial Hemp Navigating the Zodiac: Through the Green Cosmos

-Astrological Hemp: Aligning The Stars with Earth's Ancient Herb

-The Astrological Guide to Hemp: Stars, Signs, and Sacred Leaves

-Green Growth: Innovative Marketing Strategies for your Hemp Products and Dispensary

-Cosmic Cannabis

-Astrological Munchies

-Henry The Hemp

-Zodiacal Roots: The Astrological Soul Of Hemp

- **Green Constellations: Intersection of Hemp and Zodiac**

-Hemp in The Houses: An astrological Adventure Through The Cannabis Galaxy

-Galactic Ganja Guide

Heavenly Hemp

Zodiac Leaves

Doctor Who Astrology

Cannastrology

Stellar Satvias and Cosmic Indicas

Celestial Cannabis: A Zodiac Journey

AstroHerbology: The Sky and The Soil: Volume 1

AstroHerbology:Celestial Cannabis:Volume 2

Cosmic Cannabis Cultivation

The Starry Guide to Herbal Harmony: Volume 1

The Starry Guide to Herbal Harmony: Cannabis Universe: Volume 2

Yugioh Astrology: Astrological Guide to Deck, Duels and more

Nightmare Mansion: Echoes of The Abyss

Nightmare Mansion 2: Legacy of Shadows

Nightmare Mansion 3: Shadows of the Forgotten

Nightmare Mansion 4: Echoes of the Damned

The Life and Banishment of Apophis: Book 2

Nightmare Mansion: Halls of Despair

Healing with Herb: Cannabis and Hydrocephalus

Planetary Pot: Aligning with Astrological Herbs: Volume 1

Fast Track to Freedom: 30 Days to Financial Independence Using AI, Assets, and Agile Hustles

Cosmic Hemp Pathways

How to Become Financially Free in 30 Days: 10,000 Paths to Prosperity

Zodiacal Herbage: Astrological Insights: Volume 1

Nightmare Mansion: Whispers in the Walls

The Daleks Invade Atlantis

Henry the hemp and Hydrocephalus

10X The Kidney Friendly Diet

Cannabis Universe: Adult coloring book

Hemp Astrology: The Healing Power of the Stars

Zodiacal Herbage: Astrological Insights: Cannabis Universe: Volume 2

Planetary Pot: Aligning with Astrological Herbs: Cannabis Universes: Volume 2

Doctor Who: Convergence Protocol – The Replicator War

Nightmare Mansion: Curse of the Blood Moon

The Celestial Stoner: A Guide to the Zodiac

Cosmic Pleasures: Sex Toy Astrology for Every Sign

Hydrocephalus Astrology: Navigating the Stars and Healing Waters

Lapis and the Mischievous Chocolate Bar

Celestial Positions: Sexual Astrology for Every Sign

Apophis's Shadow Work Journal: **:** A Journey of Self-Discovery and Healing

Kinky Cosmos: Sexual Kink Astrology for Every Sign

Digital Cosmos: The Astrological Digimon Compendium

Stellar Seeds: The Cosmic Guide to Growing with Astrology

Apophis's Daily Gratitude Journal

Cat Astrology: Feline Mysteries of the Cosmos

The Cosmic Kama Sutra: An Astrological Guide to Sexual Positions

Unleash Your Potential: A Guided Journal Powered by AI Insights

Whispers of the Enchanted Grove

Cosmic Pleasures: An Astrological Guide to Sexual Kinks

369, 12 Manifestation Journal

Whisper of the nocturne journal(blank journal for writing or drawing)

The Boogey Book

Locked In Reflection: A Chastity Journey Through Locktober

Generating Wealth Quickly:How to Generate $100,000 in 24 Hours

Star Magic: Harness the Power of the Universe

The Flatulence Chronicles: A Fart Journal for Self-Discovery

The Doctor and The Death Moth

Seize the Day: A Personal Seizure Tracking Journal

The Ultimate Boogeyman Safari: A Journey into the Boogie World and Beyond

Whispers of Samhain: 1,000 Spells of Love, Luck, and Lunar Magic: Samhain Spell Book

Apophis's guides:Witch's Spellbook Crafting Guide for Halloween

Frost & Flame: The Enchanted Yule Grimoire of 1000 Winter Spells

The Ultimate Boogey Goo Guide & Spooky Activities for Halloween Fun

Harmony of the Scales: A Libra's Spellcraft for Balance and Beauty

The Enchanted Advent: 36 Days of Christmas Wonders

Nightmare Mansion: The Labyrinth of Screams

Harvest of Enchantment: 1,000 Spells of Gratitude, Love, and Fortune for Thanksgiving

The Boogey Chronicles: A Journal of Nightly Encounters and Shadowy Secrets

The 12 Days of Financial Freedom: A Step-by-Step Christmas Countdown to Transform Your Finances

Sigil of the Eternal Spiral Blank Journal

A Christmas Feast: Timeless Recipes for Every Meal

Holiday Stress-Free Solutions: A Survival Guide to Thriving During the Festive Season

Yu-Gi-Oh! Holiday Gifting Mastery: The Ultimate Guide for Fans and Newcomers Alike

Holiday Harmony: A Hydrocephalus Survival Guide for the Festive Season

Celestial Craft: The Witch's Almanac for 2025 – A Cosmic Guide to Manifestations, Moons, and Mystical Events

Doctor Who: The Toymaker's Winter Wonderland

Tulsa King Unveiled: A Thrilling Guide to Stallone's Mafia Masterpiece

Pendulum Craft: A Complete Guide to Crafting and Using Personalized Divination Tools

Nightmare Mansion: Santa's Eternal Eve

Starlight Noel: A Cosmic Journey through Christmas Mysteries

The Dark Architect: Unlocking the Blueprint of Existence

Surviving the Embrace: The Ultimate Guide to Encounters with The Hugging Molly

The Enchanted Codex: Secrets of the Craft for Witches, Wiccans, and Pagans

Harvest of Gratitude: A Complete Thanksgiving Guide

Yuletide Essentials: A Complete Guide to an Authentic and Magical Christmas

Celestial Smokes: A Cosmic Guide to Cigars and Astrology

Living in Balance: A Comprehensive Survival Guide to Thriving with Diabetes Insipidus

Cosmic Symbiosis: The Venom Zodiac Chronicles

The Cursed Paw of Ambition

Cosmic Symbiosis: The Astrological Venom Journal

Celestial Wonders Unfold: A Stargazer's Guide to the Cosmos (2024-2029)

The Ultimate Black Friday Prepper's Guide: Mastering Shopping Strategies and Savings

Cosmic Sales: The Astrological Guide to Black Friday Shopping

Legends of the Corn Mother and Other Harvest Myths

Whispers of the Harvest: The Corn Mother's Journal

The Evergreen Spellbook

The Doctor Meets the Boogeyman

The White Witch of Rose Hall's SpellBook

The Gingerbread Golem's Shadow: A Study in Sweet Darkness

The Gingerbread Golem Codex: An Academic Exploration of Sweet Myths

The Gingerbread Golem Grimoire: Sweet Magicks and Spells for the Festive Witch

The Curse of the Gingerbread Golem

10-minute Christmas Crafts for kids

Christmas Crisis Solutions: The Ultimate Last-Minute Survival Guide

Gingerbread Golem Recipes: Holiday Treats with a Magical Twist

The Infinite Key: Unlocking Mystical Secrets of the Ages

Enchanted Yule: A Wiccan and Pagan Guide to a Magical and Memorable Season

Dinosaurs of Power: Unlocking Ancient Magick

Astro-Dinos: The Cosmic Guide to Prehistoric Wisdom

Gallifrey's Yule Logs: A Festive Doctor Who Cookbook

The Dino Grimoire: Secrets of Prehistoric Magick

The Gift They Never Knew They Needed

The Gingerbread Golem's Culinary Alchemy: Enchanting Recipes for a Sweetly Dark Feast

A Time Lord Christmas: Holiday Adventures with the Doctor

Krampusproofing Your Home: Defensive Strategies for Yule

Silent Frights: A Collection of Christmas Creepypastas to Chill Your Bones

Santa Raptor's Jolly Carnage: A Dino-Claus Christmas Tale

Prehistoric Palettes: A Dino Wicca Coloring Journey

The Christmas Wishkeeper Chronicles

The Starlight Sleigh: A Holiday Journey

Elf Secrets: The True Magic of the North Pole

Candy Cane Conjurations

Cooking with Kids: Recipes Under 20 Minutes

Doctor Who: The TARDIS Confiscation

The Anxiety First Aid Kit: Quick Tools to Calm Your Mind

Frosty Whispers: A Winter's Tale

The Infinite Key: Unlocking the Secrets to Prosperity, Resilience, and Purpose

The Grasping Void: Why You'll Regret This Purchase

Astrology for Busy Bees: Star Signs Simplified

The Instant Focus Formula: Cut Through the Noise

The Secret Language of Colors: Unlocking the Emotional Codes

Sacred Fossil Chronicles: Blank Journal

The Christmas Cottage Miracle

Feeding Frenzy: Graboid-Inspired Recipes

Manifest in Minutes: The Quick Law of Attraction Guide

The Symbiote Chronicles: Doctor Who's Venomous Journey

Think Tiny, Grow Big: The Minimalist Mindset

The Energy Key: Unlocking Limitless Motivation

New Year, New Magic: Manifesting Your Best Year Yet

Unstoppable You: Mastering Confidence in Minutes

Infinite Energy: The Secret to Never Feeling Drained

Lightning Focus: Mastering the Art of Productivity in a Distracted World

Saturnalia Manifestation Magick: A Guide to Unlocking Abundance During the Solstice

Graboids and Garland: The Ultimate Tremors-Themed Christmas Guide

12 Nights of Holiday Magic

The Power of Pause: 60-Second Mindfulness Practices

The Quick Reset: How to Reclaim Your Life After Burnout

The Shadow Eater: A Tale of Despair and Survival

The Micro-Mastery Method: Transform Your Skills in Just Minutes a Day

Reclaiming Time: How to Live More by Doing Less
Chronovore: The Eternal Nexus
The Mind Reset: Unlocking Your Inner Peace in a Chaotic World
Confidence Code: Building Unshakable Self-Belief
Baby the Vampire Terrier
Baby the Vampire Terrier's Christmas Adventure
Celestial Streams: The Content Creator's Astrology Manual
The Wealth Whisperer: Unlocking Abundance with Everyday Actions
The Energy Equation: Maximize Your Output Without Burning Out
The Happiness Algorithm: Science-Backed Steps to Joyful Living
Stress-Free Success: Achieving Goals Without Anxiety
Mindful Wealth: The New Blueprint for Financial Freedom
The Festive Flavors of New Year: A Culinary Celebration
The Master's Gambit: Keys of Eternal Power
Shadowed Secrets: Groundhog Day Mysteries
Beneath the Burrow: Lessons from the Groundhog
Spring's Whispers: The Groundhog's Prediction
The Limitless Mindset: Unlock Your Untapped Potential
The Focus Funnel: How to Cut Through Chaos and Get Results
Bold Moves: Building Courage to Live on Your Terms
The Daily Shift: Simple Practices for Lasting Transformation
The Quarter-Life Reset: Thriving in Your 20s and 30s
The Art of Shadowplay: Building Your Own Personal Myth
The Eternal Loop: Finding Purpose in Repetition
Burrowing Wisdom: Life Lessons from the Groundhog
Shadow Work: A Groundhog Day Perspective
Love in Bloom: 5-Minute Romantic Gestures
The Shadowspell Codex: Secrets of Forbidden Magick
The Burnout Cure: Finding Balance in a Busy World
The Groundhog Prophecy: Unlocking Seasonal Secrets
Nog Tales: The Spirited History of Eggnog

Six More Weeks: Embracing Seasonal Transitions
The Lumivian Chronicles: Fragments of the Fifth Dimension
Money on Your Mind: A Beginner's Guide to Wealth
The Focus Fix: Breaking Through Distraction
January's Spirit Keepers: Mystical Protectors of the Cold
Creativity Unchained: Unlocking Your Wildest Ideas in 2025
Manifestation Mastery: 365 Days to Rewrite Your Reality
The Groundhog's Mirror: Reflecting on Change
The Weeping Angels' Christmas Curse
Burrowed in Time: A Groundhog Day Journey
Heartbeats: Poems to Share with Your Valentine
Dino Wicca: The Sacred Grimoire of Prehistoric Magick
Courage of the Pride: Finding Your Inner Roar
The Lion's Leap: Bold Moves for Big Results
Healthy Hustle: Achieving Without Overworking
Practical Manifesting: Turning Dreams into Reality in 2025
Jurassic Pharaohs: Unlocking the Magick of Ancient Egypt and Dino Wicca
The Happiness Equation: Small Changes for Big Joy
The Confidence Compass: Finding Your Inner Strength
Whispers in the Hollow: Tales of the Forgotten Beasts
Echoes from the Hollow: The Return of Forgotten Beasts
The Hollow Ascendant: The Rise of the Forgotten Beasts
The Relationship Reset: Building Better Connections
Mastering the Morning: How to Win the Day Before 8 AM
The Shadow's Dance: Groundhog Day Symbolism
Cupid's Kitchen: Quick Valentine's Day Recipes
Valentine's Day on a Budget: Love Without Breaking the Bank
Astrocraft: Aligning the Stars in the World of Minecraft
Forecasting Life: Groundhog Day Reflections
Bleeding Hearts: Twisted Tales of Valentine's Terror
Herbal Smoke Revolution: The Ultimate Guide to Nature's Cigarette Alternative

Winter's Wrath: The Complete Survival Blueprint for Extreme Freezes.

The Groundhog's Shadow: A Tale of Seasons

Burrowed Insights: Wisdom from the Groundhog

Sensual Strings: The Art of Erotic Bondage

Whispered Flames: Unlocking the Power of Fire Play

Forgotten Shadows: A Guide to Cryptids Lost to Time

Six Weeks of Secrets: Groundhog Day's Hidden Messages

Shadows and Cycles: Groundhog Day Reflections

The Art of Love Letters: Crafting the Perfect Message

Romantic Getaways at Home: Turning Your Space into Paradise

Purrfect Brews: A Cat Lover's Guide to Coffee and Companionship

The Groundhog's Wisdom: Timeless Lessons for Modern Life

The Shadow Oracle: Groundhog Day as a Predictor

Emerging from the Burrow: A Journey of Renewal

The Language of Love: Learning Your Partner's Love Style

Authorpreneur: The Ultimate Blueprint for Writing, Publishing, and Thriving as an Author

Weathering the Seasons: Groundhog Day Perspectives

Valentine's Day Magic: A Guide to Romantic Rituals

The Shadow Chronicles: Stories of Groundhog Day

Love and Laughter: Fun Games for Valentine's Day

AstroRealty: Unlocking the Stars for Property Success

The Groundhog's Path: A Guide to Seasonal Balance

Groundhog Day Diaries: Reflections in the Shadow

The Groundhog's Light: Illuminating the Path Ahead

Valentine's Traditions from Around the World

AI Wealth Revolution: Unlocking the Trillionaire Mindset

Love Rekindled: Reigniting Passion in Relationships

Single and Thriving: Self-Love on Valentine's Day

Emerald Legends: Mystical Tales of Ireland

Green Alchemy: Harnessing Nature's Magic
The Hearts of Horror: A Valentine's Day Nightmare
The Leprechaun's Guide to Wealth and Wisdom
Dancing with the Sidhe: Celebrating the Otherworld
Shamrocks and Shadows: Mysteries of the Green Isle
Emerald Energy: Harnessing Luck and Growth
The Gingerbread Golem's Valentine: A Sweetheart's Guide to Love and Enchantment
The Celtic Knot: Weaving Life and Destiny
Green Fire: Elemental Magic for St. Patrick's Day
Clover Chronicles: Finding Your Inner Luck
Ireland's Mystical Creatures: A Field Guide
Gingerbread Golem's Love Almanac
Prowl and Thrive: The Lion's Guide to Success
Love Alchemy: Transforming Your Life Through Heart Energy
WORLD DOMINATION: Woman's Rule 3:The New Life
The Midnight Rose: A Guide to Lunar Love Spells
The Forbidden Letters: Writing Your Own Love Prophecy
Luck and Lore: St. Patrick's Day for Modern Mystics
The Green Path: A Pagan Celebration of Renewal
The Dark Architect's Guide to Reprogramming Reality
Prankster's Paradise: A Guide to Harmless Hijinks
Manifest Your Reality: The Law of Attraction Simplified
The TARDIS Owner's Manual: Understanding the Doctor's Ship: *A complete guide to the TARDIS, its technology, secrets, and mysteries*
Starlit Romance: Astrology Secrets for Finding True Love
The Time Lord's Atlas: A Complete Guide to the Whoniverse: ***A breakdown of the locations, planets, and dimensions explored in Doctor Who***
Sweetheart Shadows: The Dark Side of Love and Attraction
February Fire: Reigniting Passion in Every Area of Life

The Self-Love Toolkit: 5 Ways to Embrace Who You Are
February Sparks: Ignite Your Dreams in 28 Days
March to Success: A 31-Day Action Blueprint
Ancient Paths: The 13 Sacred Principles of Dino Wicca
Echoes of Tomorrow: Navigating the AI Revolution
The Wellness Blueprint: Balancing Mind, Body, and Soul
Green Horizons: Sustainable Living for a Better Tomorrow
The AI Wealth Code: How to Make Millions with Automation
AI-Powered Creativity: Writing, Art, and Music for Profit
Extinction Rites: Rebirthing Your Soul Through Prehistoric Magick
Sacred Serpents tarot
Celestial Enchantment blank journal
Star Strains
Culinary Journeys: Exploring Global Flavors at Home
The Hollowvale Curse
The Hollowvale Harvest
The Egg of Transformation: Awakening Your Inner Power
Blooming Into Power: A Wiccan Guide to Spring Awakening
The Nightmare Nexus: The Third Doctor's Perilous Haunting
Digital Detox: Reclaiming Your Life in a Connected World
Ostara's Path: Walking the Spiral of Renewal
The Sacred Hare
Financial Freedom: Building Wealth in the Modern Age
Spring's Cauldron: Stirring the Waters of Change
The Hollowvale Pact
Quantum Consciousness: The Science of Reality Shifting
The Hollowvale Hunger
The Sacred Waters Within: A Witch's Guide to Hydrocephalus Magick
The Raven's Nest: Building a Life of Unshakable Stability
AI and the Human Mind: The Future of Intelligence
The Hollowvale Reckoning

Timeless Love: Building and Maintaining Lasting Relationships

The Raven's Roar: Unlocking Unstoppable Confidence

Raven Sight: Awakening Intuition and Inner Wisdom

The Butterfly Effect: Small Changes, Big Transformations

Taming the Boogeyman: How to Conquer Your Inner Fears

The Magick of Green: Awakening Earth's Energy in You

The Entrepreneurial Mindset: Secrets to Business Success

The Hollowvale End

The Shadow Luck Ritual: Reclaiming Power from Your Dark Side

Spring Magick for Beginners: A Simple Guide to Seasonal Energy Work

Doctor Who: The Hollowvale Conundrum

The March of Miracles: Unlocking Synchronicities in Spring

Unveiling the Cosmos: A Guide to Stargazing and Space Exploration

The Ultimate Guide to Surviving an Economic Collapse

The AI Gold Rush: How to Profit from the AI Revolution

Bastet's Shadow: The Hidden Power of Feline Magick

The Bastet Codex: Unlocking the Goddess's Magickal Secrets

Purring Spells: Harnessing Bastet's Healing Frequencies

Bastet's Nine Lives: Rebirth, Transformation, and Immortality Spells

Primal Currents: Hydrocephalus Magick in the Path of Dino Wicca

The Digital Gold Rush: Mastering E-Commerce and Online Sales

Future Shock: Adapting to the Next Decade of Change

The Quantum Mindset: Think Like a Billionaire

Sacred Motherhood: Awakening the Divine Feminine Within

The Mother's Spellbook: Enchantments for Love, Protection, and Prosperity

The Witch's Guide to Parenting: Raising Empowered and Intuitive Children

The Magick of Motherhood: Reclaiming Your Power Through Rituals

The Pagan Path to Self-Love: A Goddess's Guide to Worth and Confidence

Wild Woman Magick: Unleashing Your Primal Power

The Money Magnet Blueprint: Unlocking Unlimited Wealth

Biohacking 101: Unlock Your Body's Full Potential

The Wild Father: A Pagan Guide to Strength and Wisdom

The Sacred Masculine: Unlocking Your Inner Power

The Druid's Compass

The Warrior's Mindset

The Father's Fire

Odin's Path

Ancestral Bonds

The House That Whispers

The Magician's Code

The Wild Hunt

The Green Man's Path

The Altar of Success

The Shadow and the Sword

The High Priestess's Guide to Energy Healing

The Lunar Mother

The Sacred Self-Care Grimoire

The Womb Wisdom Codex

The Wheel of the Mother

The Witch's Guide to Manifestation

The Q2 Reset

The Ultimate Guide to AI-Powered Passive Income

Escape the 9-5

AI Feline Fortunes

The Tear-Stained Grimoire

Razorblade Runes
Cemetery Sirens
The Midnight Wristwatch
The Town That Forgets
AI Horror & Creepypasta
The Hollow Frequency
The Breach Echo
The Quiet Between Worlds
The Sigil of Tharan-Khul
Summon the Vault of Y'ha'ten
The Becoming Codex
The Profit of Az'ra-nar
The Drowned Logos
Echoes of the Eldritch Will
The Deep Ledger
Necronomicon of Networth
Covenant of the Wealthwyrm
The Whisperer's Manifesto
The Rites of Azh-K'luth
The Ark of the Crawling Coin
The Tithe of Shadows
Inkheart Abyss
The Timewinds of Y'ha-nthlei
The Spiral Labyrinth of Azag-Nirrh
The Gallifreyan Heresy of the Black Pharaoh
The Psalms of Nyog-Sotha
Black Rain Alchemy
The Infinite Maw
The Entropic Blueprint
The Oracle of Sh'guul
The Book of Breach
The Drowned Saint's Testament
Dreamcraft of the Sleeper God

The Silence Market
Cthonomics: The Dark Wealth Algorithm
Invocation of the Ten-Eyed King
Wealthbound to the Wyrm Below
Become the Unnameable
Codex of the Sovereign Flame
Rituals of Relentless Becoming
The Shadow Ascends
The Eyes Beneath You
The Will That Wakes Worlds
Silence Is a Weapon
The Mirror That Screams
The Whisper Between Moments
The Mind That Devours Fear
The Myth of the Finished Self
The Architect of Your Madness
The Voice You've Buried
The Discipline of Madness
Stormborn: Awakening Your Inner Tempest
The Mind That Ate Time
Unbind Your Becoming
The Pact You Owe Yourself
The Devourer's Diet
The Acid That Carves the Path
The Tower You Must Burn
The Breath Between Worlds
Speak Like the Deep
The Labyrinth Within
The Spine of the Sea God
Rejection Is a Portal
The Crown You Refused
The Scar Is the Spell
The Lightless Flame

The Habit of Becoming Horrific
ChickenJockey Chaos
The Gatekeeper Within
You Are Not Your Name
The Compass of the Mad
The Archive of Unsent Letters
What the Mirror Can't Show You
The Knife You Needed
Worship Nothing, Become Everything
The Other Voice
The Body the World Forgot
The Vein of the Void
The Black Bone Codex
The Puzzle of the Hidden Self (Millennium Puzzle)
The Eye That Sees the Lie *(Millennium Eye)*
The Ring of Return (Millennium Ring)
The Rod of Relentless Will ***(Millennium Rod)***
The Tally of the Soul (Millennium Tauk/Necklace)
The Key to the Locked Timeline (Millennium Key)
The Scale of Sacred Decisions (Millennium Scales)
Inferno Bites: The UnOfficial Minecraft Lava Cookbook
Rot in the Attic
Prana: The Hidden Force of Your Infinite Self
The Shadow Realm Within: Transforming Darkness Into Destiny
The Borderland Collapse
Claws of Protection: Bastet's Defensive Magick
Mr. Ring-a-Ding's Madness
Yugioh Astrology: Celestial Deckcraft and Duel Destiny (2026–2027 Edition)
The Seal You Signed: Unlocking the Power You Once Feared
The Puzzle of Infinite Minds: Unlocking the Mentalism Hidden Within

The Eye That Mirrors the All: Secrets of Inner Reflection
Doctor Who: The Toymaker's Broadcast
The Rod of Eternal Flow: Commanding the Currents of Vibration
Golden Eyes of Bastet: Enhancing Psychic Vision
The Key of Dual Forces: Balance Within the Polarity
The Scales of Living Rhythm: Timing the Dance of Life
The Necklace of Hidden Cause: Weaving the Webs of Fate
The Ring of Secret Masters: Rising Through the All Within All
Daggers of the Dying Deep
Bastet's Wealth and Fortune Magick: Prosperity Rituals of the Goddess
The Tide that Speaks
The Scrolls of Petosiris: 13 Rituals from the Feathered Eye
Petosiris and the Living Plague of Osirion
Feline Fire: Bastet's Passion and Love Magick
The Star Altar of Petosiris
Bastet's Whiskers: Supernatural Sensory Magick
The Bastet Grimoire
Feeding the Shadows
The Mouthless Prayer
The Spiral Wound
Becoming the Ibis: Lessons from Petosiris's Mind
The Crimson Coven: Cola Magick for Sweet Dominion
Sacred Cat's Paw
The Soda Zodiac: A Flavor for Every Sign
Covenant of the Crawling Flame
The Ink of Ish'Zur
Frothroot: The Thirst That Ate the World
The Golden Glyphs of Prosperity
The Etherbind Codex
Echoes of the Resistance: Reclaiming the You That Survived

Harnessed Minds: Breaking Free from Mental Control
The Eyes in the Smoke
Rootwake: The Carbon Covenant
Skitter Logic: Unlearning the Fear That Built You
Doctor Who: The World That Froths
Rootwake: The Fizz That Rewrites Flesh
Rootwake: Frothfather of the World
The Holly Pact: Blood Beneath the Mistletoe
The 2nd Mass Principle: Building Unbreakable Tribes
Web of Wits: A Survival Guide to Encounters with Anasi the Spider (Aunt Nancy)
The Hexbreaking Handbook: Effective Spells to Remove Curses
Pop Alchemy: Transform Your Life One Sip at a Time
The Mason Code: Leading in Unleadable Times
Petosiris and the Fifth Chamber of Thoth
The Ether Seed Within
The Parent of Tomorrow
Petosiris's Pyramid of Perpetual Wealth
Unlearn the World
Grimoire of the Hollow Tongue
Zodiac Weeds: Finding Your Strain Through the Stars
Aquarius Rises in the Bank
The Sugar God's Smile
The Skinclock Reversal: Biohacking the Face of Time
Debtburn: How to Obliterate What You Owe Forever
The Ice Cream Oracle: What Your Cone Says About Your Future
Silence Is Sovereignty: The Power of Being Unreadable
The Wind That Whispers Through Stone
Path of the Four Directions
Doctor Who: The Maestro's Symphony of Endings
Oxygen Grail: Breathing to Undo the Clock

Zodiacal Collapse: When Stars Devour Time
Teachings from the Red Sand Silence
Doctor Who: Omega – The Broken Equation
Memory Wipe Your Past: Start Over Like a MiB
Mitochondria Prime: Ignite the Core of Youth
A Nest of Roaches
Grub from the Galaxy: MiB Recipes You'll Never Forget
Whiskers of Power: Bastet's Guide to Inner Sovereignty
The Gift Must Cost Them: Negotiation Through Unequal Exchange
The Worm Guys' Wealth Code: Hustle Like an Alien
Bug Out: The Edgar Method for Ruthless Goal Setting
Weaving Life with Spiderwoman's Pattern
Doctor Who: The Rani's Renaissance
How to Get a Job (If You're a Puppygirl)
Speak Through Others: The Art of Proxy Power
T-Rex Your Trauma: Reclaim the Power of Your Primal Self
The Black Briefcase: How MiB Stay Wealthy in Silence
The Thirst Beyond Reason: Understanding Diabetes Insipidus From the Inside Out
Backwoods Witchcraft for Billionaires: The Pagan Path from Dirt Roads to Gold Roads
The Moonshine Grimoire: Fermented Spells for Abundance
The Nameless Geometry
The Wraith's Mixtape: Spellcasting with Songs of Sorrow
The Gallifreyan Gentleman: Silent Wealth, Sonic Confidence, and the Doctor's Code of Living
Sugar Water Confidence
Dino Totems: Spirit Guides from Earth's First Gods
Pumpkin Sigils & Ritual Smoke
The Hózhó Compass
The Distortus Discipline – Order from Inner Mutation
Witchcraft for the Cold-Blooded Soul

Moonlight Over the Blessingway
Water, Interrupted: When the Body Forgets How to Hold On
Deformed but Divine: Embracing Your Asymmetry
Hexes in the Henhouse: The Farm Witch's Guide to Power
The Reversed Flame: A Grimoire of Inverted Power
Salt, Cells, and Sanity: Reclaiming Balance with Diabetes Insipidus
King of the Broken: Crowning the Flawed Self
Moonlight Scars: Emo Moon Magick and the Art of Lunar Sorrow
Noose Spells: Magick of the Hanging Rope
The Goth Cathedral: Rituals of the Broken and Beautiful
The Cretaceous Codex: Dino Spirits and Fossil Magick
The Turkey Bones Ritual
Nine Lives of Manifestation: Unlocking Bastet's Reality Codes
Chaos Muscles: Building Strength from Twisted Pain
Emo Blood Magick: The Veins of Power
The 3AM Flood: Nighttime Urination, Sleep Loss, and the DI Spiral
The Silence Between the Stars
The Lemon Method: Sour Your Way to Success
Starlit Sovereign
The Rite of Twelve Gates: Walking the Gates of the Duat.
Cornbread and Conjure: Recipes for Riches and Rootwork
The Black Rose Rituals: Emo Love Spells and Obsession Magick
The Eternal Goodbye: Death Magick and Rebirth Rituals
Sinkrot: The Drain That Remembers
The Hybrid Mindset: Thinking Beyond Evolution
Bone Dry: Navigating Dehydration Before It Breaks You
Wreathcraft: Winter Sigils and Yuletide Spells
The Rite of Twelve Mouths

S'mores of the Damned: Haunted Recipes for Halloween Night

Rethink the Drink: A Beverage Survival Guide for DI Warriors

The Shadow Chord: Guitar Magick and Sonic

Malformed Yet Majestic: Leading When You Feel Wrong Inside

The Cursed Diary: Ink-Stained Spells of the Emo Soul

Anxiety Off Switch: Emergency Reset for a Fried Nervous System

The Energy Heist: How to Take Back Your Life from Drainers

Beyond the Bathroom: Rebuilding Your Social Life With DI

Coyote's Gift for Decision Makers

Ghoul-Goo: Spooky S'mores You'll Die For

Echoes in the Mirror: Scrying and Self-Destruction Magick

Thread and Thorn: Stitching Spells from Rural Cloth

The Mogwai Mind: Building Untouchable Wealth from Small Ideas

Be Your Own Guide: Trust Your Inner Compass

Hormones in Chaos: The Endocrine Puzzle of Diabetes Insipidus

ChronoCleanse: Detox Your Biological Timeline

The Limb You Hide Is the One That Saves You

Leaves, Bones, and Whisper Spells

The Dinosaur Mindset: Prehistoric Tactics for Modern Wealth

Clawing Back Control: A Bastet Method for Boundaries and Empowerment

Sambain Codes of the Forgotten

Orange Alchemy: The Autumnal Spellbook

Monster Within, Master Without

The Sigil That Sleeps

Hearthcraft: Yule Hearth Sigils and Winter Warmth Spells

Temple of the Purring Moon: Rituals from Bastet's Lineage
When the Earth Remembers Your Footsteps
Food for Mood: Eat to Heal Depression, Not Just Survive It
Witch of the Kudzu Vine: Southern Pagan Wealth Secrets
The Invisible Diagnosis: Advocating for Yourself With DI
The Coffin's Lullaby: Sleep Magick and Nightmares as Portals
Ashes of the Will: Rituals for Erasing the Self
The Fracture Rite: Shattering the Magickal Core
Funeral Candles: The Art of Emo Flame Magick
The Black Grimoire: A Blank Ritual for Writing in Absence
Phantom Thirst: A Halloween Survival Guide for Diabetes Insipidus
The Hollow Crown: Emo Royalty and Magick of the Outcast King
Sandpainting for the Soul
Falling Into Balance: Using the Extra Hour to Recalibrate Life
100 Southern Superstitions That Still Work
The DI Child: A Parent's Guide to Raising Hydrated, Happy Kids
The Jungle of Shame: Escaping the Hidden Lab of Doubt
The Witch's Toast: S'mores Spells and Creepy Confections
The Hoodoo Pantry: Spells from the Mason Jar
The Immortal Fortune: Secret Wealth Lessons from Captain Jack Harkness
The Specter's Embrace: Magick for Channeling Ghostly Lovers
Grateful Waters: A Thanksgiving Survival Guide for Diabetes Insipidus
The Seizure Gospel
Harvestbind: Autumn Sigils and Samhain Spells
Doctor Who: The Algorithmic Awakening
Silent Nights, Steady Waters: A Christmas Survival Guide for Diabetes Insipidus

The Extra Hour Effect: How One Hour Can Transform Everything

Blade Between the Breaths

Running with the Mountain Shadows

Echoes of the Failed Experiment – Becoming a Living Legacy

Swamp Witches & River Ghosts: Real Southern Hauntings

Cornbread Prophecies: Magical Recipes from a Southern Table

Doctor Who: The Signal in the Star

Bloomcraft: Spring Sigils and Equinox Enchantments

Vanisher: How to Disappear from the Internet Without Losing Your Life

The Ultimate Christmas Cookie Cookbook

The Unbreakable Parent: How to Mentally Survive Raising Kids in a Broken World

Time Debt: How to Reclaim the Hours You Didn't Know You Lost

One Month, One Million: Unconventional Cash Creation Tactics

Doctor Who: The Cyber Conversion Protocol

Black Friday Frenzy: The Art of Finding Hidden Online Deals

The Grimoire Buried Under the Apple Tree

Digital Couponing Masterclass: Your Step-by-Step Guide to Black Friday Savings

The Fire Inside the Flint

Shadows on the Ceiling: The Emo Guide to Astral Magick

The Bone-Eaters Beneath Us

Black Friday Bundle Blueprint: Creating Irresistible Product Packages for Maximum Sales

Thirteen Nights of Unbinding

Doctor Who: Engines of Influence

Pumpkin Spice Alchemy: Recipes of Fire and Frost

When Raptor Met Rexy: Prehistoric Lessons in Wild Romance

Oblivion's Candle: Burn the Path Behind You

Campfire Curses and Chocolate: A Halloween S'mores Grimoire

The Wallet That Wasn't Mine: Breaking Free from Inherited Scarcity

The Cola Zodiac: What Your Fizz Says About Your Fate

Frostfire Fortune: Unlocking Winter's Hidden Prosperity

Signal Jamming: Detox Your Brain from Info Overload

The Dust of the Forgotten Rite

The Golden Cat Sigils: Drawing Power in Bastet's Name

Mud Magick: The Prosperity of Getting Dirty

Savory Spicefall: Beyond the Pumpkin Pie

Pumpkin Spice Apothecary Kitchen

The Pumpkin Spice Economy: Turning Trends into Billions

The Ember Veil: 13 Nights of Fire Magick

Financial Freeze: When Earning Triggers Panic

The Gingerbread Alchemist: Sweet Recipes with a Twist

Biosynth Power: Programming Yourself from Scratch

Echoes from the Talking Circle

Truffle Alchemy: Fungus of Fortune

Spores of Power: The Truffle Witch's Handbook

Doctor Who: The Tower That Speaks

The Mycelium Veil: Truffle Magick Unbound

Broke But Ashamed: Healing the Shame Wound of Debt

The Evergreen Mind: Growth Through Winter Stillness

The Black Veil Truffle Rite

The Voice Beneath Symbols

Witchlight on the Bayou: Swamp Spells for Sovereignty

I Grew Up Poor and Now I Sabotage My Success

The Lantern of Hollow Souls

Shutdown Survival: A Citizen's Guide to Thriving When Government Stops

When Abundance Feels Like a Threat: Healing the Hidden Fears of Enough

The Scarecrow Grimoire

Owls of the October Veil

Candlewax and Curses: A Halloween Spellbook

Excavating the Inner Fossil – Transforming Fossilized Thoughtforms into Tools of Power

The Yule Witch's Spellbook: Magick for the Holiday Season

Haunted Christmas: Ghost Stories for Winter Nights

The Christmas Survival Guide: Thriving Through the Chaos

The Bone Orchard Rites

Haunted Commerce: The Ghost in the Marketplace

When Money Triggers the Inner Child

Silent Night with the Silence: A Christmas Thriller

The Lightning Crown: Living and Leading Through Seizures

TARDIS Tidings: Festive Stories from the Whoniverse

Autumn Reset: Slowing Down Without Falling Behind

The Trillion Dollar Soul: Rewriting the Currency of Reality

Truffle Eclipse Magick

Micro-Manifestations: Quick Magick That Works

5-Minute Rituals for Busy Witches

The Marshmallow Massacre: Halloween Treats with a Sinister Twist

Blood and Blackberry Thorns

Magickal Mornings: Rituals for a Blessed Christmas Day

Embers of the All-Hallows Fire

The Pumpkin Market Collapse

The Hour You Gained: Transforming Time Into Power

The Chamber Must Be Sealed: Mastering the Power of Controlled Access

The Cursed Manuscript of Petosiris

The Festive Hearth: Creating Holiday Traditions
Darkness Rising: Thriving as Nights Grow Longer
Harvesting Time: Turning the Year's End Into Your New Beginning
Petosiris and the 13th Zodiac Key
Wagewound: When Paychecks Become Identity Prisons
Walls That Watch
The Silent Feast: Rituals of Power in the Longest Night
The Distortus Legacy : Becoming a Deformed King in a Perfect World
The Hollow Masks
The Gratitude Furnace: Forging Gold from Thanks
Feast of Inner Gold: Eating for Energy and Enlightenment
Haunted Commerce: The Season of Spending Spirits
Fear Bonds: How Panic Creates Profit
Black Friday E-Commerce Playbook: Sales Tactics to Skyrocket Your Holiday Revenue
Budgeting for Black Friday: A Holiday Savings Planner
Haunting the Harvest Moon
The Warrior's Water: Emergency Preparedness for People With DI
The First Sip of the Year: A New Year's Survival Guide for Diabetes Insipidus
Doctor Who: The Thirteenth Node
The Unseen Struggle: Mental Health, Anxiety, and Chronic Thirst
The Hearth's Hidden Ledger: Counting Energies as Currency
The Gift Alchemist: Turning Any Offering Into Gold
The Papyrus of the Bound Spirit
The Magick of Leftovers: Transmutation in the Fridge
Frost and Fortune: Christmas Wealthcraft for the Modern Magus
Last-Minute Gifts: Creative Ideas on a Budget

10 Secrets to Surviving Holiday Crowds
The Witch's Dow Jones
The Witches' Graveyard Shift
Pumpkin Sigils: Carving Rites for Midnight Power
The Secret Shopper's Black Friday Guide: How to Get Early Access and VIP Deals
Fever in the Foundation
The Neuralyzer Reset: Reprogram Your Morning Routine
Lightning Lessons of the White Painted Woman
The Enchanted Snowflake
The Magic Sip: Surviving Disney Parks with Diabetes Insipidus
The One Who Draws Through You
Santa's Secrets: A Magical Holiday Planner
Silent Bells, Loud Miracles: Self-Help for the Season of Stillness
The Sugar Spell Codex: Confectionary Magick of Christmas
Autumn Hexcraft: Fallen Leaves, Fallen Barriers
Sleep Like a Fortress: Build a Life Where Insomnia Can't Survive
Nowhere Was Ever Home
Christmas Under the Stars: A Celestial Holiday Guide
Rentproof: How to Never Be Evicted Again
Workless: Escape the 9-5 Without Being Broke
The Gilded Gift: A Wealth Altar for Christmas Morning
The Black Friday Grimoire
The Hollowing: Ceremonies of Spiritual Collapse
Doctor Who: The Nameless Signal
Where the Eagle Hides His Courage
The Dwarf Tyrant's Ascent: Claiming Power in a World of Giants
The Currency of the Dead: Trading with Spectral Bankers
The Icebound Witch: Survival and Magick in the Cold

The Emergency Money Mind: Constant Crisis, Zero Calm

Thirst & Roses: A Valentine's Survival Guide for Diabetes Insipidus

Springing Into Clarity: Mastering the Energy Shift of Daylight Saving

Speed of the Nanotyrant: Agile Strategies for Life's Hunt

The 90-Day Reset: A Science-Backed Guide to Reinvent Yourself Before the New Year

The Coil of Thorns

Timegates Unleashed

Dopamine Fasting 2.0: Rewiring Your Brain in a World of Overstimulation

The Nanotyrannus Mutation: Embracing Your Differentiated Form

Unwritten January: How to Use the Blank Page of the Year to Re-Author Your Life

Feast of the Forgotten Spirits: Ancestor Magick for the Holidays

The Burnout Codex: A System for Thriving Beyond Stress

I Don't Deserve to Have Money

When the King Doesn't See You: The Shadow Predator's Guide

The Reset Ritual :A Guide to Shedding Last Year's Weight—Emotional and Physical—by Spring Cleaning Your Soul

Calendar Alchemy: Learn to Bend Time and Productivity around Your Natural Rhythms

The Mirror Contract: A One-Sentence Agreement with Yourself that Unlocks Real Change

The Nile Formula: Sacred Flow for Millionaire Minds

Forward Momentum: Productivity Rituals for the Lost Hour

Harvest Gold: Wealth Magick of Pumpkin Spice Commerce

The Magick of Christmas Lights: Illuminating Holiday Rituals

Cranberry Crown: Royal Self-Worth through Ritual Meals
Petosiris and the Worms of the Feathered Throne
The Evergreen Equation: Self-Help for Sustained Growth
The Rain Will Wash Us Away: Emo Weather Magick
Snowlight Shadows: Magick Under Frozen Stars
Doctor Who: Merger of Empires
The Light Within the Feast: Magickal Wealth of Yuletide Flame
Momentum Machines: Small Habits Designed to Snowball into Unstoppable Forward Motion
Calm Spells: Magickal Solutions for Anxiety Relief
Santa's Final List: The Naughty Never Leave
The Mystic's Guide to Banishing Worry
The Silence Dividend: Turning Quiet Mornings into Compounding Growth All Year
Charmed Stillness: Rituals to Ease the Mind
Blood Spiral Ascension
The Vanishing Heart Invocation
Crystal Calm: Harnessing Stones for Anxiety
The Nano Tyrant Code: Strength in the Small Predator
The Energy Ledger: Accounting Methods for Vitality, Not Just Money
Snowglobe Mindset: Shake Up Your Thoughts, Settle Into Peace
The Weight of the Feather: Anubis's Codes for Soul Balance
Pocket Peppermint Power: Tiny Rituals for Big Holiday Energy
Shadowkeeper of the Golden Jackal: Anubis's Path to Energetic Protection
The Witch's Breath: Anxiety Relief Through Magickal Breathing
The Tiny Ember: Pocket Motivation for Cold Days

The Twelfth Doctor: The Rebel with a Cause (Peter Capaldi, 2013–2017)

The Thirteenth Doctor: Breaking the Mold
(Jodie Whittaker, 2017–2022)

The Fourteenth Doctor: A New Beginning (David Tennant, 2022–2023)

The Fifteenth Doctor: Rewriting the Stars
(Ncuti Gatwa, 2023–2025)

Santa's Shortcut to Success: Micro Habits for a Better New Year

The Midnight Cocoa Manifesto: Comfort Rituals for Hard Nights

Why I Can't Save: Trauma Blocks to Financial Planning

Dino Brain, Mega Goals: Rewire Yourself for Savage Success.

Jurassic Profit: Unearth Your Inner Millionaire Fossil

Scales & Softness: Dating with Dino Heart

Carnotaurus Dreams.

Red Willow Thinking.

Reindeer Resilience: How to Keep Going When You're Exhausted

Candlewick Courage: Lighting Strength in Dark Seasons.

Elf-Mode Focus: Fast Attention Fixes for Busy Seasons

Futureproof Feelings: Emotional Skill-Building for Resilience No Matter What the New Year Brings

The 90-Day Rewire: Transform Your Neural Pathways Before Spring Blooms

Jolly Rich: Christmas Micro-Money Magick for Fast Prosperity.

Gingerbread Gratitude: Mini Practices for a Happier Holiday

Trauma-Spending: When Money Becomes a Drug

Goal Skeletons: Build Minimalist Frameworks for Resolutions That Last

The Snarl Strategy: Growling Back at a World That Silenced You

The Hourglass Reset: Reclaiming What the Clock Took

Yule Claw: Dino Rites of Light in the Darkness

Sacred Circles: Grounding Rituals for Anxious Souls

Clockstopper's Gut: Rebuilding the Core of Time

Winterfire Drive: Harness the Cold Season's Stillness to Ignite Deep Motivation

The 5-Minute Productivity Hack: Small Steps to Big Results

Light Ascending: A Self-Help Guide to Longer Days

Inner Economy: Trade Self-Doubt for Confidence Like a High-Value Currency

Simple Success: Decluttering Your Life for Better Results

The Resilient Mind: Thriving in Tough Times

The 2026 Playbook: Mastering the Year Ahead

The Spring Sleep Solution: Conquering Fatigue After Time Change.

The Hormonal Compass: Navigate Back to Your Youth

Golden Vision: Eating for Your Eye Color with the Power of Ghee

Lionhearted Love: Strength in Relationships

MiB Mindset: Think Like a Cosmic Agent

The Ladder of Small Wins: Climb Out of Stagnation by Stacking Micro-Victories

The Momentum Hour: Gaining More in Less Time.

The Year of You: A Self-Help Blueprint for Unapologetic Self-Ownership

The Dust That Watches You Back.

The Astral Parent

Shadow of the King: The Nanotyrannus Parable

Tiny Tidings of Triumph: Small Wins That Change Your Life

Dwarf Tyrant Rising: When You're the One They Overlook

The Bank Account Mirror: Healing How You See Yourself Through Money

Cretaceous Black

When Love Costs Too Much: Romantic Triggers and Financial Wounds

Dream-Eater's Guide to Wealth

Unzipped Reality: The Jacket That Opens Portals

The Power of No: How to Set Boundaries and Get Rich

Keeper of the Desert Veil: Anubis's Teachings on Illusion & Truth

Redacted Stargates: Stories the SGC Buried

The Clock That Dripped Time

Doctor Who: The Silent Acquisition

Hairline Manifestation: Unlocking Power at the Edge of Thought

Cash-Eater Crickets: How Insects Predict Economic Collapse

Dead Pet Whisperer: Grief Alchemy from the Other Side

The Love Algorithm Is Broken: Hack Romance Before It Hacks You

The Rite of the 8-Limbed Seal

Melt the Moon: A Fire Ritual to Reshape Emotion

Venomous Miracles: Healing Through the Poison Path

Wealth Without Water: The Post-Aquatic Rich Life

The Butterfly Betrayal: When Change Turns on You

The Quiet Upgrade: How Humans Are Secretly Rebuilding Themselves Without Asking Permission

Nobody Taught Us This: The Missing Human Manual for Money, Energy, and Self-Respect

You Were Never Broken: Why Most People Are Reacting Normally to an Unstable World

After the Noise Ends: How Humans Reset When the World Finally Goes Quiet

The Month That Tells the Truth: Why January Reveals What the Rest of the Year Hides

Tremors Party Unleashed: The Ultimate Guide to a Graboids Birthday Bash

Cold Start Human: Rebooting Motivation Without Forcing Momentum

The Year that doesn't start until they say

Love Without Performance: What Connection Looks Like When No One Is Watching

February Is a Mirror: What Love Exposes About You

How We Learned Love Wrong: Uninstalling Cultural Myths About Connection

You Are Not Too Much: Why Needing Love Is Not a Flaw

The Crooked Fence Covenant: Backwoods Boundaries and Witch Wealth

The Day That Keeps Repeating: Why Your Life Feels Stuck—and How to Shift It Gently

Nothing Changes Until Something Softens: Escaping Repetition Without Violence to Yourself

Same Life, Different Ending: How Tiny Choices Rewrite Repetition

The Loop Isn't Punishment: Why You're Being Asked to Learn, Not Suffer

Panic at the Register: Retail Anxiety and Public Shame

The Secret Formula to Becoming an Influencer in 90 Days

The New Rich: How to Retire by 35

Digital Nomad Secrets: How to Travel the World and Make Millions

Burn Your Waiting Room: Escape the Delay Spiral

Strapped for Pleasure: A Complete Guide to Pegging and Strap-On Play

Locked in Desire: A Guide to Chastity Play and Intimate Control

Burrowing into History: Groundhog Day Through the Ages

The Shadow Forecast: The Science of Groundhog Day

Choice Cascades: How One Decision in January Sets Ripples for the Whole Year

The Anti-Anxiety Blueprint: Mastering Fear and Stress for Success

The Ancestral Path of the Jackal Priest

Winterborn Titans: Giants of Ice and Stone

The Extinction Spire

The Emotion That Made Me Millions

Delete Their Voice: Become Unreachable

The Frostbound Mysteries: Mythical Beings of January's Chill

The Roar Within: Unlocking Your Potential

From Burrow to Sky: Groundhog Day Explained

The Boogey Book: Festive Ward-Off Edition

Fooled Ya! The Psychology Behind Great Pranks

April Fools' Alchemy: Transforming Everyday Items into Pranks

Anchor Habits: Root Yourself in Unshakable Routines That Endure Seasonal Change

Emerald Waters: A St. Patrick's Day Survival Guide for Diabetes Insipidus

The Groundhog's Legacy: Myths, Legends, and Facts

Six Weeks of Mystery: The Truth Behind Groundhog Day

The Upgrade Mind: Tech-Like Patches and Updates for Your Mental Operating System

Moon Blood, Star Flesh: Embracing Your Hybrid Nature

Groundhog Lore and Legend: A Complete Guide

You Are the Lie They Can't Kill

Download a Different Reality

The Quiet Advantage: Winning Without Announcing Yourself

A Year of Gratitude: Unlocking Joy

Touch Grass: A Pagan Reset for a Burned-Out Digital World
Cold Start Wealth: Building Financial Power from a Standing Still Point
Astrology Without Fate: Using Cycles Without Surrendering Control
The Future is Remote: Work Less, Earn More, Live Anywhere
Harvest of Silence
The Algorithm Knows Your Name
April Fools' Day for Introverts
Soft Power Systems: Influence That Doesn't Exhaust You
Practical Magick for Real Life: Focus, Intent, and Follow-Through
January Is a Lie: Designing Momentum Without the Calendar
Universal Flow: Managing DI in High-Energy Theme Parks
Electric Allure: Exploring Erotic Electro-Play
The Masked Embrace: Exploring Sensory Deprivation
The Ultimate April Fools' Survival Guide
Splashproof Survival: Waterparks & Wave Pools with DI
Agile Predator, Still King: Crafting Your Speed in a World That Celebrates Size
The Shadow Feast: Groundhog Day's Sinister Side
The Bug's Business Model
Edge of Bliss: Mastering the Art of Tease and Denial
Midnight Alchemy: Rituals for Transformation Between the Old Year and the New
Punxsutawney Bloodlines: A Groundhog Day Horror
The Burrower: Groundhog Day's Darkest Secrets
Buried Alive: A Groundhog Day Horror Story
Blood Moon Markets: The Witch's Guide to Wealth Magick
The Groundhog's Shadow: What It Means for the World
Seasonal Shadows: The Groundhog Day Phenomenon
The Shadow's Curse: A Groundhog Day Horror Tale
Punxsutawney Revealed: A Guide to Groundhog Day

Safari Hydration: Zoo & Wildlife Park Survival for DI
The Foolproof Prank Planner
Latex Lust: Embracing Fetish Fashion **is a sophisticated**
Whip & Whisper: The Dynamics of Impact Play
The Shadow Burrow Chronicles: Horror Beneath the Ground
Frozen Shadows: A Groundhog Day Thriller
The Groundhog's Revenge: A February Nightmare
Burrow of the Damned
Everyday Enchantment: Magickal Practices for Modern Living
Budget Bliss: The Easy Path to Financial Freedom
Six More Weeks of Terror
The Oxygen Debt
The Ice Veil: Mystical Beasts of January's Shadows
Roots That Remember
Polar Myths: Creatures of the Icy Abyss
The Marginalia Covenant
AI and the Occult: Digital Spirits, Sigils, and Cyber-Witchcraft
Roleplay Realms: Crafting Fantasies and Scenes
The Last Clean River
Lover in the Shadows: A Groundhog Day Tale
Buried Hearts: A Groundhog Day Gothic Romance
Anubis Wept for Petosiris
The Lantern Knows Your Name
Rituals of the Last Shadow
The Bell That Rings for No One
Shadows of Love and Death
The Groundhog's Bride: A Dark Valentine's Tale
Frozen Kisses: A Horror Romance for Groundhog Day
The Creative Spark: Igniting Your Passion Projects
From Cub to King: A Journey of Transformation
Six Weeks to Midnight: A Groundhog Day Romance
Tide of the Unclean

Burrow of Desire: A Groundhog Day Paranormal Romance

The Shadow Magick Almanac: Harnessing Groundhog Day Energies

AI for Emo Influencers: Growing an Online Following Without the Anxiety

AI for the Melancholy Millionaire: Making Money Without Social Interaction

Winter's Grip: A Horror Romance Beneath the Frost

Shadowed Hearts: A Love Buried in Winter's Chill

The Shadow Lover: A Groundhog Day Gothic Love Story

Beneath the Burrow: A Groundhog Day Thriller

The Punxsutawney Conspiracy

The Crimson Pact: Emo Blood Oath Magick

The Shadows of Gallifrey: A Doctor Who Horror Collection

Whispers in the Vortex: Chilling Tales from the TARDIS

www.ingramcontent.com/pod-product-compliance
Lightning Source LLC
LaVergne TN
LVHW022012200926
848481LV00007B/2356
* 9 7 9 8 2 9 5 5 6 4 6 2 8 *